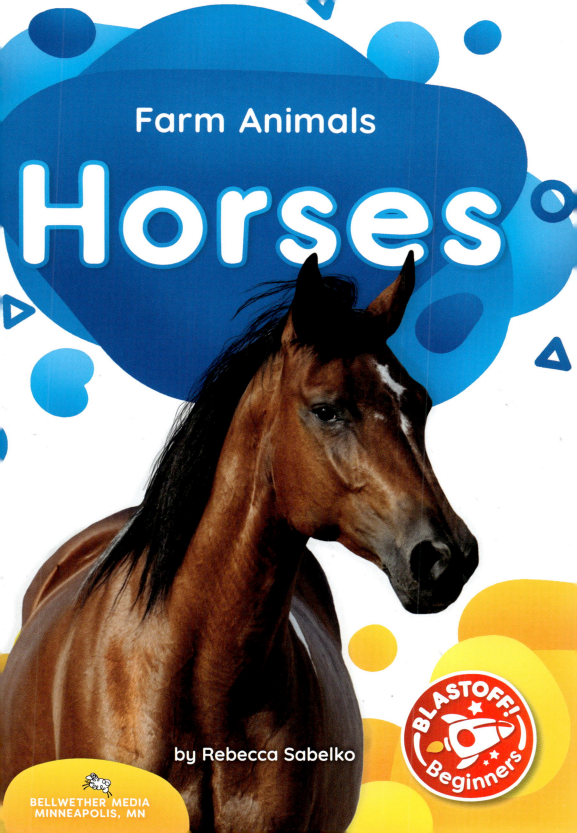

Blastoff! Beginners are developed by literacy experts and educators to meet the needs of early readers. These engaging informational texts support young children as they begin reading about their world. Through simple language and high frequency words paired with crisp, colorful photos, Blastoff! Beginners launch young readers into the universe of independent reading.

Sight Words in This Book

a	eat	many	they
and	get	of	to
are	have	play	too
be	in	ride	up
big	like	run	
can	long	their	

This edition first published in 2024 by Bellwether Media, Inc.

No part of this publication may be reproduced in whole or in part without written permission of the publisher. For information regarding permission, write to Bellwether Media, Inc., Attention: Permissions Department, 6012 Blue Circle Drive, Minnetonka, MN 55343.

Library of Congress Cataloging-in-Publication Data

Names: Sabelko, Rebecca author.
Title: Horses / by Rebecca Sabelko.
Description: Minneapolis, MN : Bellwether Media, 2024. | Series: Blastoff! Beginners: Farm Animals | Includes bibliographical references and index. | Audience: Ages 4-7 | Audience: Grades K-1
Identifiers: LCCN 2023039750 (print) | LCCN 2023039751 (ebook) | ISBN 9798886877625 (library binding) | ISBN 9798886879506 (paperback) | ISBN 9798886878561 (ebook)
Subjects: LCSH: Horses--Juvenile literature. | Farm life--Juvenile literature.
Classification: LCC SF302 .S23 2024 (print) | LCC SF302 (ebook) | DDC 636.1--dc23/eng/20230831
LC record available at https://lccn.loc.gov/2023039750
LC ebook record available at https://lccn.loc.gov/2023039751

Text copyright © 2024 by Bellwether Media, Inc. BLASTOFF! BEGINNERS and associated logos are trademarks and/or registered trademarks of Bellwether Media, Inc.

Editor: Elizabeth Neuenfeldt   Designer: Laura Sowers

Printed in the United States of America, North Mankato, MN.

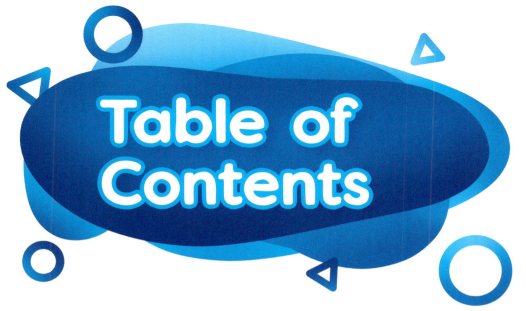

Table of Contents

Fast Runners	4
What Are Horses?	6
Life on the Farm	14
Horse Facts	22
Glossary	23
To Learn More	24
Index	24

Fast Runners

Horses run in a field. They are fast!

field

What Are Horses?

Horses are big farm animals. They can be many colors.

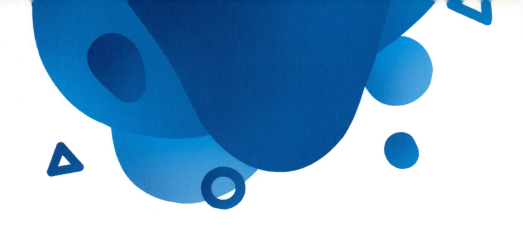

Horses have long faces. Their pointed ears stick up.

Horses have thick **manes**. They have long tails.

Horses have long legs. They have strong **hooves**.

hooves

Life on the Farm

Farms can be big. Farmers ride horses to get around.

farmer

Horses move **herds** of animals.

herd

Horses play in fields. They rest in **stables**.

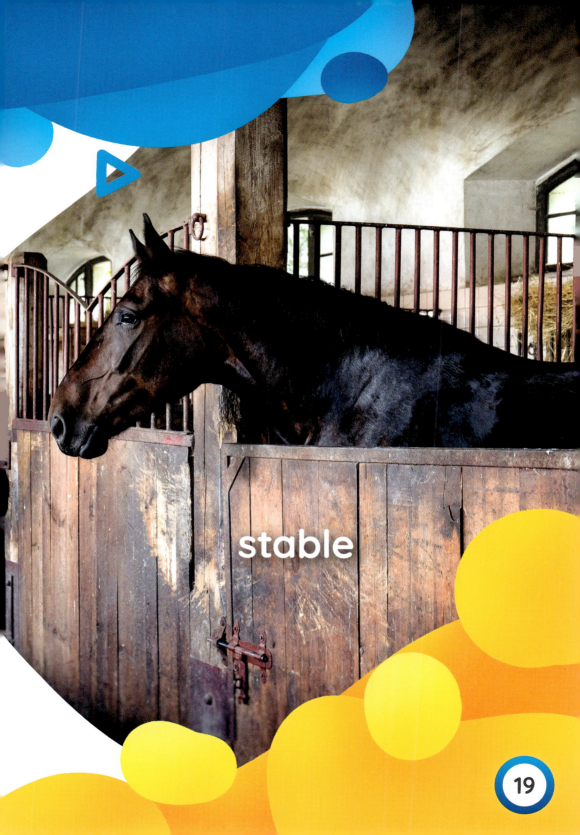
stable

Horses eat grass and hay. They like apples, too. Neigh!

grass

hay

apples

Horse Facts

Parts of a Horse

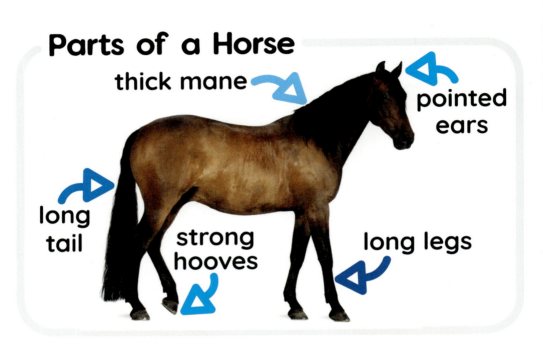

- thick mane
- pointed ears
- long tail
- strong hooves
- long legs

Life on the Farm

carry farmer

move herds of animals

rest in stable

Glossary

herds

large groups of animals such as cows or sheep

hooves

hard coverings on the feet of horses

manes

long, flowing hair on the necks of horses

stables

buildings with stalls where horses live

To Learn More

ON THE WEB

FACTSURFER

Factsurfer.com gives you a safe, fun way to find more information.

1. Go to www.factsurfer.com.

2. Enter "horses" into the search box and click 🔍.

3. Select your book cover to see a list of related content.

Index

apples, 20, 21
colors, 6
ears, 8, 9
eat, 20
faces, 8
farmers, 14, 15
farms, 6, 14
field, 4, 5, 18
grass, 20
hay, 20, 21
herds, 16, 17
hooves, 12
legs, 12
manes, 10, 11
play, 18
rest, 18
ride, 14
run, 4
size, 6
stables, 18, 19
tails, 10, 11

The images in this book are reproduced through the courtesy of: Kwadrat, cover; Eric Isselee, pp. 3, 9, 22; Viktoriia Bondarenko, p. 4; Erica Hollingshead, pp. 4-5; SunnyMoon, pp. 6-7; Olga Salt, p. 8; Rita_Kochmarjova, pp. 10-11, 18; Usanee, p. 12; Makarova Viktoria, pp. 12-13; Vanessa van Rensburg, pp. 14-15; LifeJourneys, pp. 16-17; ewg3D, pp. 18-19; Mr. Meijer, p. 20 (grass); Volodymyr Burdiak, pp. 20-21; Oleksiichik, p. 21 (hay); PK Studio, p. 22 (carry farmer); nattrass, p. 22 (move herds of animals); ARDIELPHOTO.COM, p. 22 (rest in stables); majeczka, p. 23 (herds); Zanna Pesnina, p. 23 (hooves); Callipso88, p. 23 (manes); Alxddd000, p. 23 (stables).